FEMALE
SPORTS STARS

CHELSEA HOUSE PUBLISHERS

FEMALE
SPORTS STARS

SUPERSTARS OF WOMEN'S BASKETBALL

J. Kelly

CHELSEA HOUSE PUBLISHERS
Philadelphia

CHELSEA HOUSE PUBLISHERS

Produced by Daniel Bial Agency and Associates
New York, New York

Senior Designer   Cambraia Magalhães
Picture Research   Sandy Jones
Cover Illustration   Bill Vann
Frontispiece photo: women playing basketball, circa 1900

3 5 7 9 8 6 4

Library of Congress Cataloging-in-Publication Data

Kelly, J.
    Superstars of women's basketball / J. Kelly.
      p.   cm. — (Female sports stars)
    Includes bibliographical references and index.
    Summary: Profiles the lives and basketball careers of Ann Meyers,
Nancy Lieberman, Cheryl Miller, Sheryl Swoopes, and Rebecca Lobo.
    ISBN 0-7910-4389-4 (hardcover)
    1. Women basketball players—United States—Biography—Juvenile
literature. [1. Basketball players. 2. Women—Biography.] I. Title. II. Series.
GV884.A1K45 1997
796.323'092'2—dc20
    [B]   96-34781
                                                                  CIP
                                                                   AC

CONTENTS

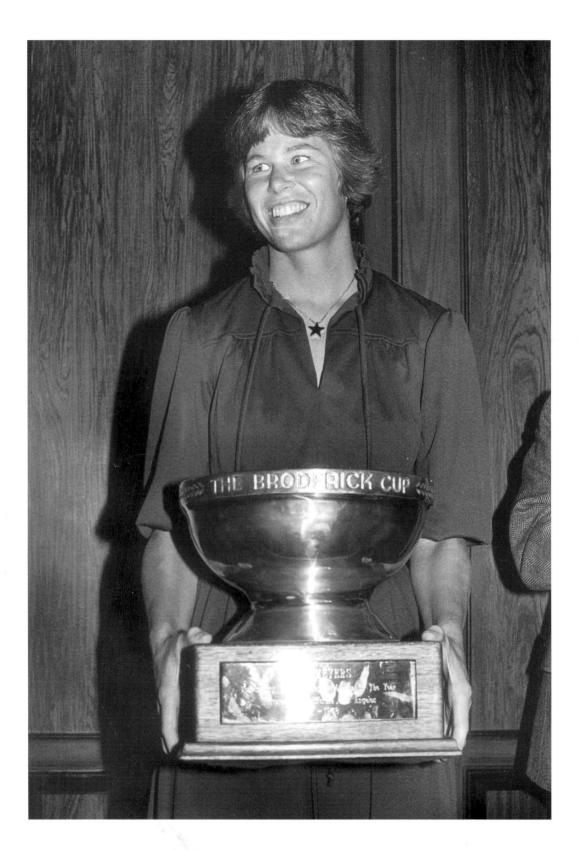

1

ANN MEYERS: THE PIONEER

Sports, and basketball in particular, was a big part of the family life of Ann Meyers. "We're an athletic family and everybody plays basketball," said Meyers, one of 11 children. "There was always somebody to play with."

Ann's father, Bob, played college basketball at Marquette University in Milwaukee, Wisconsin, and had a brief career in the pros. Her older sister also played college basketball, and her brother, Dave, four years older than Ann, was an All-American at UCLA and then went on to a successful career with the Milwaukee Bucks of the NBA. Dave grew to 6'8", while Ann never topped 5'9", making it somewhat of a mismatch when the two played. "Dave helped me with my shooting," Meyers said. "But he wasn't much good to play one on one."

In the fifth and sixth grades, Meyers played on the boys' team in La Habra, California, and

Ann Meyers shows off the Broderick Cup, an award for being named the outstanding collegiate woman athlete of 1977-78.

each of those years her teams won elementary school championships. In junior high, however, coed teams were not allowed, even though Meyers had no fear of playing with the boys. "I wanted to play with the guys," she said, "but there was opposition from the coach and a lot of petty arguments about showers and stuff."

Meyers played on the girls' team at Sonora High in La Habra when she was a freshman in 1971 and was named the team's most valuable player. In 1972, she transferred to Cornelia Connelly High School in Anaheim, where she again was the team MVP. The next year, as a junior, she returned to Sonora to lead her team as its captain and MVP. By her senior year in 1974, girls were eligible to play on the boys' team, and Meyers wanted badly to compete with them. She looked forward to the challenge of playing on a higher level. "I know I would have made the team," she said, "but a lot of people discouraged me. My brother Dave felt it would put a lot of pressure on the coach." So Meyers decided not to try out for the boys' team. "I'll regret it the rest of my life," she said at the time.

Ann's skills in high school as a scorer, passer, and ball handler became known around the country. When she was a senior in high school, she was selected to play on the U. S. national girls' team. It was the first time a high school player was selected to play on the national team—just the first in Meyers' life full of firsts.

While Meyers was gathering accolades in high school, her brother Dave was playing for UCLA and helping the Bruins capture national championships. At the time, the UCLA men's teams were legendary. Coached by John Wooden and with stars like Marques Johnson,

*Ann Meyers (left) hopes
for a rebound as her
greatest opponent,
Carol Blazejowski
(right), of Montclair
State, tries a layup.
Meyers and UCLA beat
Montclair State in this
1978 AIAW semifinal
game.*

Kareem Abdul-Jabbar, Bill Walton, and Gail
Goodrich, the Bruins were a college basketball
dynasty. But the women's program at UCLA, as
it was at so many colleges, was considered second class. Budgets were geared primarily
toward men's sports. Scholarships to play girls'
basketball simply were not awarded.

All that changed with the arrival of Ann
Meyers on campus. She was the first woman at

UCLA to receive a full basketball scholarship. By granting a woman a basketball scholarship at such a high profile school as UCLA, a new respect was born for women's basketball. Some of that second-class status was beginning to be shed.

In 1975, her freshman year at UCLA, Meyers led the team in scoring, rebounds, assists, and shooting percentage. UCLA finished with a 20-4 record, and Meyers was honored by making the All-American team that year, the only freshman to do so. "It came as a big surprise to me that I was selected to the team," Meyers said modestly.

The following year, 1976, was not only another stellar one for Meyers at UCLA—she led the team in rebounds, steals, and assists—it was also a year in which the Olympics were held. Meyers become part of a U.S. team that included another budding superstar and rival, Nancy Lieberman.

Throughout her basketball career, Lieberman, a flashy guard from New York, was contrasted with the smooth, fundamentally precise Meyers from California. It was as if the two players represented different types of basketball: the aggressive playground style of the East Coast versus the laid-back style of the West Coast. The two players were completely different even in appearance: Meyers was the cool blonde, while Lieberman was the fiery redhead. "I play a very fundamental game. I can't spin a basketball on my finger or indulge in the flashy, between-the-legs dribble like others do. I don't need those things," said Meyers, fueling the fire of their rivalry.

For the Olympics, however, the two women put their differences aside and played together, helping the U.S. women's team capture a silver medal. The gold medal that year went to the Soviet Union, the perennial power in international women's basketball. But it wouldn't be long before a shift of power occurred, and the U.S. women became the dominant team.

Meyer's final year at UCLA was her most magical one. She had already been selected All-American each of her first three years. But there was one accomplishment at UCLA Meyers had yet to fulfill: to win a national championship. Her chance came when the Bruins met the Maryland Terrapins in the title game of the AIAW (Association for Intercollegiate Athletics for Women) tournament. During the regular season, UCLA had lost to the Terrapins, 92-88; but that game was played on Maryland's home court. This one was played at Pauley Pavilion, UCLA's arena. And the result was different, with UCLA winning, 90-74, and tearing down the nets in celebration of its first national championship.

In the win, Meyers played a brilliant all-around game, scoring 20 points, handing out 9 assists, pulling down 10 rebounds, and making 8 steals.

"People ask me what it's like to play in Annie's shadow," said Meyers' teammate Heidi Nestor after the game. "Annie is such a completely unselfish player that she casts no shadow. She's so good she doesn't need to."

The Maryland game was the finale of her college basketball career, but the honors kept coming for Meyers. For the fourth time in her four years at UCLA, she made the All-American team, and in 1978 she was also named the UCLA Athlete of the Year. Other significant honors for Meyers in 1978 included the Broderick Award for Outstanding Collegiate Basketball Player and the Broderick Award for

Outstanding Collegiate Female Athlete. To cap it all off, her college uniform number 15 was retired in the Basketball Hall of Fame in Springfield, Massachusetts.

Her college career over, Ann Meyers didn't have the option her brother Dave had, which was to go on to a pro career. In 1978, there were no professional women's leagues, so after collecting all her awards, Meyers remained at UCLA to earn her degree in sociology and com-

Meyers shows off her free-throw shooting form as Indiana Pacers coaches watch in the background.

pete as a high jumper on the track team and to star on the women's volleyball team. She continued to play basketball; she just didn't have a league to play in.

Then, in September 1979, Sam Nassi, the new owner of the Indiana Pacers, held a press conference to announce the signing of Ann Meyers to a guaranteed, one-year contract. With the signing, Meyers became the first woman to ever sign with an NBA team.

The signing created an uproar and was greeted with more than its share of criticism and skepticism. How does a 5'9", 135-pound woman go up against men a foot taller and 100 pounds heavier? "It's a stunt, like Bill Veeck signing a midget when he owned a baseball team," said Sam Schulman, owner of the Seattle SuperSonics.

"It's disgraceful, a travesty," added Sonny Werblin, president of Madison Square Garden, which owned the New York Knicks.

And from Dick Vitale, who was then head coach of the Detroit Pistons: "There is no way she can play at this level."

Even her brother Dave, who was playing for the Milwaukee Bucks, had his doubts. "I know that the Pacers' attendance was not good last year," Dave said. "This could be an investment in advertising."

But Bob Leonard, coach of the Pacers, disputed the skeptics. "We are looking at Ann as a super athlete with credentials worthy of a free agent's contract," Leonard said. "Believe me this is no gimmick on our part."

Ann Meyers certainly didn't look at the signing as a gimmick but as a challenge, one she welcomed. She was also surprisingly confident. "I can dribble and make plays as well as anybody in the league," Meyers said. "I have played against

Calvin Murphy, Wilt Chamberlain, Julius Erving, and other male pros in pick-up games at UCLA and in Las Vegas and have held my own."

There were believers out there as well as doubters. "I believe in equal rights and equal opportunity for all and if she is capable of playing and being an asset to the Pacers, then I will welcome her to the team. Let's give her a chance and not be narrow-minded about it," said Pacer guard Johnny Davis.

Billy Knight, another Pacer, said, "I just want to welcome her. I wish her the best and we'll see what happens."

Janet Guthrie, the first woman to drive in the Indianapolis 500 and a trailblazer herself, said, "I'm not much of a crusader, but if I paved the way for another woman to get a break, I'm happy for her."

Despite her confidence and the support of others, Meyers knew what she was getting into—that she would be competing against players bigger, faster, and more physical than she had ever competed against before. "I have a slight chance," she said, "but it's the opportunity of a lifetime. Lot's of people have dreams, and my dream has always been to make the NBA."

But just a few days later, after a preseason rookie camp, Meyers' dream ended when she was released from the team. Coach Leonard was impressed by her fundamental skills but admitted she just was not physically able to handle the competition. "If she was 6 inches bigger and 40 pounds heavier it would have been a different story," said Leonard.

Jack McCloskey, assistant coach for the Pacers, looked at it with humor. "She gave me a little peck on the cheek and a hug," said McCloskey. "It meant a lot to me. I've never gotten a kiss from a player who got cut."

Despite the sad ending to a storybook tale, Meyers was positive about the experience. "I was given the chance of a lifetime that most men don't get," she said. "I'm happy with myself. I did the best I could."

Even though she was no longer in the NBA, Meyers was not without a professional basketball league. A fledgling woman's professional league, the Women's Basketball League, had recently formed, and Meyers became one of the top picks. "What Ann Meyers did with the Pacers and the NBA really helped women's basketball," said Wanda Szeremeta, the coach of the New Jersey Gems, the WBL team

In 1993, Ann Meyers was inducted into the Basketball Hall of Fame along with (from left to right) Julius Erving, Dick McGuire, Calvin Murphy, and Bill Walton.

that signed Meyers to a three-year, $130,000 contract.

"Ann Meyers will be to the WBL what Joe Namath and others were to professional football, hockey, and soccer," said Robert J. Milo, the owner of the Gems.

But the WBL didn't last very long, and Meyers was once again a player without a league. She hoped to compete in the 1980 Olympics in Moscow, but Meyers' basketball career came to an abrupt end when the U.S., in protest of the Soviet Union's involvement in the war in Afghanistan, boycotted the 1980 games.

In 1980, 1981, and 1982, Meyers, demonstrating her tremendous athletic ability, entered ABC's "Superstars" competition and won the women's division each year. Her exposure to the media led her to a career as a broadcaster. She has since worked for ESPN, ABC, and NBC and continues to freelance as a television basketball analyst.

Probably the most significant event in Meyers' life after basketball was meeting Don Drysdale, the ex-Dodger and Hall-of-Fame pitcher who was then working as a broadcaster. The two married in 1986, and in 1988, when Meyers became the first woman to be inducted into the Basketball Hall of Fame, Drysdale and Meyers became the first husband-wife team in any of the major halls of fame. They had three children.

On July 3, 1993, at the age of 56, Don Drysdale died of a heart attack. The loss was devastating to Meyers. "Even though we had a relatively short period of time together," said Meyers, "it just rips my heart out that he's gone. He will always be the love of my life."

Since then, life for Meyers, like playing basketball with men, has been a constant challenge.

But she has approached it the same way. "I know there will be positive things that come from it," Meyers said, referring to the death of her husband. "I hope it will make me a better person and a better parent."

In any event, Ann Meyers has accomplished feats no woman basketball player ever did before. She went up against the big guys and didn't worry about being embarrassed. She wasn't awed by the challenge. But Meyers is still realistic about the odds of women competing against men; she knows that there is a long way to go before the playing field is level. "People keep saying that attitudes about women playing competitive sports with men will change in five to ten years, but they've been saying that for the last fifty years," Meyers said. Then she added, "Someday we'll make it."

NANCY LIEBERMAN:
THE AMBASSADOR

When Nancy Lieberman was a little girl, her father left home. He would visit occasionally, but soon his visits dwindled, and eventually he dropped out of the family's life. Nancy's older brother, Cliff, found a release from the pain of growing up without a father through his studies and music. Nancy found release through sports. "Sports was my escape," Lieberman said. "I didn't have to think about anything when I was fantasizing about sinking the winning free throws, stealing home, completing a hat trick."

Sports were what was sweet about Nancy Lieberman's childhood, but much to the dismay of her mother, Renee, sports were also becoming an obsession. The first sport Nancy fell in love with was football—not a game usu-

Nancy Lieberman on her way to scoring 33 points as Old Dominion University crushed Queens College, 106-53, at Madison Square Garden in 1979.

ally played by girls. "I would look out in the yard and see a pile of helmets and bodies, but no Nancy," said Renee Lieberman. "Then I realized my daughter was under all that."

Nancy also played baseball, but soon it was basketball that became her true love. She played pickup games on the playgrounds of Far Rockaway, New York, and at the local YMHA. It was during the pickup games that she learned the toughness that became her trademark. "In pickup games you learn to survive. You have to win to keep your court, and if you lose, it might take a whole day just to get your court back," Lieberman said. "That was the time of my life."

In the pickup games, she always played against boys. "The boys were always bigger and rougher, so I had to be mean and hard-nosed. I had to learn to take elbows and give them back."

Lieberman grew to 5' 10", but her jumping ability was her one weakness. To improve her vertical leap, she would constantly be jumping inside her house. "I'd stand next to a wall and jump up and slap it with my hand. I wanted to be able to jump like my hero, Dr. J., Julius Erving," said Lieberman.

Nancy's mother thought that sports was just a passing fancy, that her daughter would soon grow out of it. She was seriously mistaken. "My kid and sports, you wouldn't believe," said Renee Lieberman. "I yelled. I screamed, 'I'll murder you. Stop it already. Sports aren't for girls. Why don't you be a secretary? A nurse? Put on a dress?' Nothing worked." She even tried to put an end to Nancy's basketball playing by puncturing her basketballs with a screwdriver. "She just went out and got more balls," said Renee Lieberman. It was hopeless. Her daughter was consumed by basketball.

Nancy played on the Far Rockaway High School girls' team, and in her sophomore year she brought the team to the finals of the city championship, where they lost by one point. During her junior season, Nancy's flashy play was noticed by LaVozier LaMar, the coach of a boys' AAU team in Harlem called the New York Chuckles. He recruited Lieberman to play on his team and soon she was regularly riding the subway all the way from Queens to Harlem to play with the Chuckles.

"I had to show them I could play and get respect, so they didn't ease up on me," Lieberman said about playing with boys. And respect was what she got. Because of her aggressive style, her teammates nicknamed the red-headed Lieberman "Fire."

Tia Sossoman of Louisiana Tech is about to have a rebound taken away by the shorter Nancy Lieberman as Old Dominion teammate Anne Donovan comes over to help.

"She would roar down the court left, right, turning, spinning, flying in the air. You know, getting it all done. Everybody got to know the Fire right away, so nobody messed with her on the streets," said LaMar. "She was the queen of Harlem."

Lieberman began to get close to her teammates, who were African Americans, and started bringing them home to meet her mother. To Nancy, color was never an issue. "It didn't matter to me who I played with just as long as they wanted to win and keep the court," Lieberman said. "I couldn't understand prejudices. Maybe it was because I was a red-headed, white, Jewish tomboy. How could you expect me to understand prejudice?"

In 1974, when Nancy was 16, she was picked to try out for the United States women's basketball national team. But there was a catch: Nancy had to pay her way to Albuquerque, New Mexico, where the tryout was being held. Neither she nor her mother had that kind of money, but Brian Sackrowitz, her high school coach, organized a local fund drive and raised $1,500—enough for Lieberman to attend. It marked the beginning of international play for Lieberman, and two years later she was selected to play on the 1976 U.S. women's basketball Olympic team. At just 18, she was the youngest member of the team.

The coach of the U.S. team, Billie Moore, was impressed by Lieberman's all-around skills. "She is quick, very smart on the court, a good shooter, excellent jumper, a very, very strong rebounder, aggressive, hard-nosed, very strong on defense," said Moore at the time. "She just doesn't have a weakness. She does everything you can ask a player to do."

The 1976 Olympic team, which also featured future Hall of Famer Ann Meyers, won the silver medal. And with Nancy's success, her mother was finally won over. She realized she would never rid her daughter of her love of hoops; instead, it was Renee who converted and became Nancy's number one fan. "The woman who used to yell at me for watching sports on television all of the time began to join me in front of the set," said Nancy.

But when Nancy chose to attend Old Dominion University in Norfolk, Virginia, her mother was perplexed. "All I could picture was a sailor town and a broken-down plantation," Renee Lieberman said.

Nancy choose ODU, out of many other colleges that recruited her, because its women's basketball program was up and coming and she thought it was the perfect fit for her. "I felt ODU was just far enough away to get out of New York, but close enough so I could always get back to my environment."

Though Lieberman did well her first two years at ODU, making the All-American team in her sophomore season, it wasn't until her junior year that the team began to gel. "We've always had individual talent, but last year we used it individually," said Lieberman at the time. "Now we're working as a unit."

During that 1978-1979 season, the Lady Monarchs were 35-1 and pitted against the Lady Techsters of Louisiana Tech in the finals of the AIAW championship game. In the game, Louisiana Tech was up 32-27 at halftime, but in the second half Lieberman, along with teammate Inge Nissen, took control. ODU won the game 75-65 as Lieberman had 20 points, 7 rebounds, 7 assists, and 6 steals.

Jim Oshust, the director of the Greensboro Coliseum, where the championship game was played, compared Lieberman's style to that of David Thompson, who won a college championship five years earlier with the North Carolina State Wolfpack (and, coincidentally, 18 years later shared the stage with Lieberman when both were inducted into the Basketball Hall of Fame). "She's flashy and spectacular and you remember all that," Oshust said, "but at heart she is a total book player. She gives you fundamentals right out of the instruction guide."

After her stellar 1978-79 season, Lieberman was voted an All-American again and awarded the Wade Trophy as the best women's college basketball player in the country. The next year, Lieberman's last at ODU, the team, with a 37-1 record and 27-game winning streak, was even more dominant. In the AIAW championship game, the Lady Monarchs walloped Tennessee, 68-53. Lieberman scored only 12 points in the game but had 9 rebounds and 6 assists. Her coach, Marianne Stanley, acknowledged Lieberman's contributions. "You don't find many guards that'll rebound the way she does. You don't find many players who can completely control the tempo and complexion of the game as Nancy does," said Stanley. "I don't

Lieberman playing in the 1979 Pan Am Games.

think I've seen many people who have her con-fidence. You can't teach that. Nancy probably had that when she was born."

Lieberman was awarded another Wade Trophy after her senior season and for the third year in a row was voted onto the All-American team. She finished her career at ODU by scoring a total of 2,430 points, averaging 18.1 points a game, and had 512 steals, a school record.

After college, Lieberman's first basketball business was to lead the U.S. women's team to an Olympic gold medal in Moscow in the sum-mer of 1980. But her dreams were dashed when the U.S. boycotted the Olympics. Instead, Lieberman kept busy playing in the New York Pro Summer League; she was the only woman player in the semi-pro league. Lieberman played for the Gailyn Packers, and the men were impressed. "She's a lot better than some of the guys in the NBA," said Geoff Huston, who played with the New York Knicks and Dallas Mavericks.

"She plays with a lot of confidence," said Al Skinner, who played for the Philadelphia 76ers. "She's a real nice passer, and she knows the basics. There are guys in training camps who don't play that well."

Lieberman wasn't looking to crack the sex barrier in professional basketball, she just wanted to keep on top of her game in prepara-tion for the upcoming season in the Women's Basketball League, where she was the number one draft choice in 1980. "This is going to help me become better," said Lieberman of her work in the New York Pro Summer League.

In her first season with the Dallas Diamonds of the WBL, Lieberman's team made the playoffs, and she was named all-pro. But, to her disap-pointment, without marketing and fan support, the WBL folded. Lieberman, like so many other gifted female basketball players, was without an outlet to continue her skills. "Suddenly I felt like a college graduate who had studied hard and made the dean's list semester after semester only to find out upon graduation that there wouldn't be a job," wrote Lieberman in a 1983 editorial that appeared in the *New York Times.* "Women's professional basketball was the highest goal left for me in my sport, and it was gone in a year."

Despite her efforts, a revival of a professional women's basketball league never got off the ground. Still, basketball was in her blood. In 1986, she was offered a contract to play for the Springfield Fame of the men's United States Basketball League. She made the team and in doing so made history as the first woman in America to play in a men's professional league. But though Lieberman played with men in the New York Summer Pro League and the USBL, she never felt the need to prove herself amongst them. She recognized that the men's game was different and really not suited for the physical makeup of a woman. "If people are looking for slam dunks and 30-foot jumpers, they'll be disappointed in the women," said Lieberman. "The men are stronger and faster." All that strength and speed she was competing against in the USBL finally took its toll on her. Though she did her best to hold her own, she eventually wore down and retired from professional competition.

In 1996, Lieberman, who, after marrying Tim Cline, is now known as Nancy Lieberman-Cline, received basketball's top honor when she was inducted into the Basketball Hall of Fame in Springfield.

Lieberman-Cline now runs a sports marketing company in Dallas and has become a

In 1980, Lieberman won her second consecutive Wade Trophy, awarded to the nation's top collegiate women's basketball player.

spokesperson for the women's game. "The women's game is incredible in its own right. And exciting. Our game is execution because we're not going to overwhelm with physicality. This is why we work on our fundamental skills, dribbling and passing patterns."

She also has concerns that girls playing basketball are influenced too much by male players. "It worries me to see these girls impressed by the fighting, the trash talking, the baggy shorts. The tattoos! I make it my little mission to talk history to girls. They need to know about Cheryl Miller and Ann Meyers. Men hand their heroes down to their sons; little boys know all about Mickey Mantle and Jackie Robinson and never saw them play. Women have to do the same thing."

CHERYL MILLER: THE PERSONALITY

The Miller family is a family of exceptionally gifted athletes. There is the oldest, Saul, Jr., whom Saul Miller felt was the most talented of his children; Darrell, who went on to play baseball with the California Angels; and Reggie, now a star in the NBA. Growing up in such a family where the sons were so talented, the daughter, Cheryl, had to work extra hard to get attention. Often the brothers made it tough on her. "They'd throw me a ball, tackle me, pile on, mangle me," said Cheryl Miller. "But they were real proud of me being able to throw and kick balls and fight and stuff."

They might have been proud of her, but it still wasn't easy trying to compete with them. She knew she had talent of her own, but because of her brothers, that talent could be

Cheryl Miller (right) helps carry off coach Pat Summitt after the U.S. won the gold medal at the 1984 Olympics by beating South Korea, 85-55.

overlooked, especially by the person she most wanted to impress: her father. "It was hard to tell if Cheryl was talented," said Saul Miller, "because of all the talent around her."

Instead of retreating into a shell and hiding behind her brothers' acclaim, Cheryl went the other way. Whatever it took to grab the spotlight for herself, she did. And that usually meant playing endless games of basketball in her backyard with her brothers and father. She did whatever she could to hold her own against the boys. All her hard work quickly paid off, and by the age of 13 she was featured in newspaper article. It was just the beginning of a career of headlines for Miller and exactly what she wanted. "I loved all the attention," she recalled. "The more I received, the harder I worked."

By the time Cheryl grew to 6' 2", not only was she holding her own against her brothers, she was usually beating Reggie, who was a year younger than she. One day, however, when Cheryl woke Reggie for his daily one-on-one whipping, she noticed that when he got up, he kept getting up. "All of a sudden he was 6' 6'," said Miller. "I took first outs, blew by him like always and sailed in for the lay-up. As I was running under the basket I heard this noise. Clang. I looked up and the ball was still up there. So was Reggie. He had pinned it. I stopped in my tracks."

Soon sister and brother were no longer one-on-one combatants but a team. They even had an unusual scam going. Reggie would approach two guys playing hoops and offer a challenge. "Wanna play me and my sister for 10 bucks," he would say, while Cheryl would remain out of sight. The unsuspecting victims, thinking they had an easy mark, would gladly accept the challenge. And then Cheryl would

_Shortly after scoring
105 points in a single
game at Riverside Poly
High School, Cheryl
showed off some of
the trophies she had
already won._

come out from behind the bushes, all 6' 2" of her and, according to Reggie, "the guys would be awed."

All that training with her family paid off. At Riverside Polytechnic High School in Riverside, California, Cheryl became a basketball legend. In each of her four years in high school, she led her team to state championships. With Cheryl playing center and averaging over 36 points a game, Riverside Poly had a phenomenal 84-game winning streak.

But there were two feats she accomplished in high school that were far and away the most memorable. The first was scoring an amazing 105 points in a game against Norte Vista High. In few high school basketball games does an entire team score 105, yet Cheryl scored that all by herself. No man has ever scored that many in the NBA; Wilt Chamberlain scored 100 once, and no one else has come close.

Cheryl's other high-school feat had nothing to do with statistics, rebounds, assists, points, or free throws. She did what no woman in high school basketball had done before: she slam-dunked. And she did it more than once.

"When I dunk, it's like I'm on Cloud 15," said Miller. But dunking wasn't something that she could do anytime. "The conditions had to be just right, the game situation, the condition of the floor."

Word of Cheryl Miller's talents spread quickly, and soon colleges across the country, 250 to be exact, were wooing her. At the time, 1982, she was the most highly recruited female athlete ever. She finally chose the University of Southern California, and in keeping with her love of attention, Miller called a press conference to announce her decision.

Attending USC made perfect sense for Miller. Not only did the school have a blossoming women's basketball program, but it was also located in Los Angeles, just a few miles from the media glitz of Hollywood. She couldn't ask for a better combination.

It didn't take long for Miller to make her mark on USC women's basketball. In her freshman year at USC, the Lady Trojans went into the NCAA championship game against Louisiana Tech with a 30-2 record and ranked number two in the nation. The 31-1

Lady Techsters, with a 30-game winning streak and a margin of victory of 26.4 points were ranked number one. In the game, Louisiana Tech pulled ahead by as many as 13 in the first half; but USC, led by Miller, who scored 27 points, blocked 4 shots, had 9 rebounds and 4 steals, came back to win, 69-67. Miller was named tournament MVP for her stellar performance.

Miller's season statistics helped make her an All-American in her first year. For the season, she averaged 20.3 points per game, had 111 steals, and 75 blocked shots. But it was her unlimited energy and charisma that seemed to impress her teammates most. "Cheryl's flamboyant, and it rubs off," said teammate Pam McGee. "You see her being so vital, so dynamic, and you want to be part of it."

In 1983-84, her sophomore year, Miller's star, after her phenomenal freshman year, continued to rise. Not only was she considered one of the best players in the country, she was also becoming a very recognizable figure in the media. During the season, Miller averaged five or six interviews a week and made close to 75 television appearances. In February 1984, during the Grammy Awards show in Los Angeles, she surprised the world when, while Donna Summer was singing "She Works Hard for the Money," she ran across the stage, in front of Summer and a world-wide audience, and slam-dunked a basketball. It was all part of the act, but Miller remembers being extremely nervous about the stunt. "I was afraid the ball would bounce off my foot and hit Michael Jackson or somebody in the audience," said Miller.

All that media hype did not detract from her game. The Lady Trojans duplicated their effort of the previous year, once again winning the

Miller soars to the hoop in the finals of the 1984 Olympic Games. She led the U.S. team in scoring as it easily beat Australia, 81-47, for the gold medal.

national championship, this time defeating Tennessee, 72-61, in the final. Miller scored 16 points in the game and was voted tournament MVP for the second year in a row.

After two seasons at USC, Miller was definitely living up to the hype. But her style, that energy and charisma her teammates thrived on, did not always go over so well with the competition. She was soon branded a showboat. During games, she pointed in the faces of her competition, blew kisses to opposing benches, drop kicked balls, did arched back cheerleader flips, and even moonwalked. Most flamboyant of all was Miller's "Hotdog Wrist." After taking a long-range shot and seeing it swish through the hoop, Miller would wag her wrist on the follow through. The gesture was perceived as an "in your face" taunt, but Miller claimed that the wagging wrist came about from a technique her father taught her to help her follow through with her shots and was not meant as a taunt. In her defense, her brother Reggie, who, at the time was starring for the men's basketball team at cross-town rival, UCLA, also employed the "Hotdog Wrist," so perhaps it truly was a family thing.

Still, Miller had her detractors. "Sometimes I think Cheryl goes overboard with her theatrics," said former college basketball star Ann Meyers. "She blatantly plays to the crowd and the media."

One opposing coach called her a hot dog while another said she should major in "theatrics." Earnest Riggens, head woman's basketball coach at San Diego State, was one of her critics who seemed to soften on her style. "I'm a conservative coach," said Riggens. "I just had never seen the hot dog stuff before. But that goes over in L.A., the fans look for it. Cheryl does things to the extreme, but she's good and she knows it. I guess it's not so bad to show everybody you're good."

And Basketball Hall of Famer Nancy Lieberman, who, in her time, was also labeled a showboat, also defended Miller. "The flamboyance is her bread and butter," said Lieberman. "She sees those cameras and she seizes the moment. Sure, it's all Hollywood, but that's

O.K., too. We're going to induct her into the Prima Donna club."

During the controversy, one of her biggest supporters was her brother Reggie. "She plays like a guy," Reggie said. "That why she dominates, and that's why you like to watch her. She likes to get the crowd going."

Commenting on her style, Cheryl said, "I've never been an act. I'm always spontaneous. I'm impatient and hyper and emotional and it all comes out on the court."

When assembling the United States womaen's basketball team for the 1984 Olympics, Head Coach Pat Summit, known as a stern disciplinarian, recognized Miller's flamboyance as a crucial element of her game and, instead of making her change her style, found a way to incorporate it into her team concept. The results were remarkably successful. The team won the gold medal in Los Angeles that year, and Miller was the leading scorer. Miller considers winning the gold medal one of the most memorable moments in her career.

Miller's junior year at USC, 1984-1985, was one of her best. She averaged 26.8 points and 15.8 rebounds per game, along with 80 blocked shots, 86 assists, and 116 steals for the season. She was voted All-American for the third straight year and was Naismith player of the year and winner of the Wade Trophy for academics and community service. The team, however, lost nine games and failed to win a third straight national championship. "It was definitely a new experience for me," Cheryl said about the losing. "I've never lost so many games in my life. It was character-building. I didn't want to admit it last year, but it was a letdown after the Olympics."

After graduation, Cheryl Miller returned to USC as coach of the women's basketball team. Here she greets Jualeah Woods during the NCAA playoffs.

The following year, Miller's last at USC, the Lady Trojans once again made it to the NCAA finals. But unlike their first two appearances, USC was defeated, 97-81, by the top-ranked and undefeated University of Texas Lady Longhorns. Miller finished the game with 16 points but fouled out with over seven minutes left in the game.

Over her career at USC, Miller was a four-time All-American and three-time Naismith Award winner. She scored 3,018 points grabbed 1,534 rebounds, made 1,159 field goals, and netted 702 free throws. The team had a 112-20 record during her four years. In recognition of her achievements, Miller became the first USC basketball player, male or female, to have her number (31) retired.

Though there was no professional women's league for Miller to turn to after her college career, she graduated from USC on time and with a degree in sports information. With her degree and her sparkling personality, she landed a job with ABC Sports as a commentator for college football and men's basketball.

While she was working for ABC, she took time off to lead the U.S. team to a gold medal at the 1986 Goodwill Games in Moscow. Miller was selected to play on the 1988 U.S. Olympic women's basketball team in Seoul, South Korea, but just before the games were to begin, she was forced to withdraw because of a knee injury. She also made an attempt at the 1992 Olympics in Barcelona, but once again, injuries kept her off the team. "I always could play hurt," Miller said, "but in '88 and '92 it got to the point where just standing up was a big problem. It was over."

In 1993, Miller once again broke new ground when, at the age of just 29, she was named head woman's basketball coach at her alma mater, USC. She coached the Lady Trojans for just two seasons and has since returned to where she feels most comfortable: in front of a camera. She currently does color commentary for NBA games for Turner Broadcasting. "Being a color commentator for basketball is the greatest job in the world," said

Miller, "because now I can criticize coaches and officials without getting thrown out of the game."

In a time when women's basketball was considered bland, Cheryl Miller came on the scene and, with her effervescent, flamboyant style, changed all that. She added glitz to a game that was perceived as boring. Because of that, some, like Nancy Lieberman, consider her a revolutionary. "Of course she has revolutionized the game," Lieberman said. "She's taught young girls to play hard all the time and to be physical. I think Cheryl is the best thing that could have happened to the game."

Miller wouldn't go quite that far. "I don't call myself a revolutionary," Miller said, but then with a grin added, "I do think I'm a trendsetter."

4

SHERYL SWOOPES: THE SCORER

How many athletes have been honored by having a sneaker named after them? Michael Jordan and his Nike Air Jordans is the most famous example. But recently Nike introduced a new line of athletic footwear named in honor of another talented basketball player. This time the player, however, was female. The shoe is called "Air Swoopes," after Sheryl Swoopes.

Some people might think that the reason Nike named the shoe after Swoopes was because she had the perfect name for a basketball shoe. After all, Swoopes rhymes with hoops; it's a marketing natural. But the Oregon shoe company didn't just call their new shoe Air Swoopes because of the catchy name; they believe they found the perfect athlete to repre-

Sheryl Swoopes leaps for joy after Texas Tech defeated Ohio State for the 1993 NCAA championship. Swoopes scored 47 points in the game and was voted the tournament MVP.

sent their product: a true, modern star who will inspire other girls to play the game.

"We would have done it if her name was Smith or Jones," said Liz Dolan, vice president of marketing at Nike, of the Air Swoopes sneaker.

Keith Peters, another Nike representative added, "There is clearly a great awareness of who Sheryl is, especially to insiders in women's basketball."

You didn't have to be an insider to know what Sheryl Swoopes accomplished on the afternoon of April 4, 1993. On that day, a nationally televised audience, along with a sell-out crowd in the Omni arena in Atlanta, Georgia, got to witness one of the most amazing performances in a championship game ever displayed on a basketball court. Swoopes scored 47 points for Texas Tech in its 84-82 win over Ohio State to capture the 1993 women's basketball national championship. Everyone watching that day became aware that the 6'0" forward was much more than just a player with a catchy name.

Well before Sheryl Swoopes's shining moment in Atlanta, there were people who knew of her immense basketball-playing abilities. The first were her older brothers, James and Earl, with whom she used to play basketball when she was growing up in Brownfield, Texas. "Once you go out and play with guys, you figure you can always score off girls," said Swoopes of her games with her brothers.

At Brownfield High School, Swoopes led her team to three state championships. In her senior year, she averaged 26 points, 5 assists, and 14 rebounds and was named an All-American and Texas Player of the Year.

After graduation in 1989, Swoopes received a scholarship to the University of Texas at

*Shelley Jarrard (left)
and Rhonda Blades
(right) of Vanderbilt
University try the
impossible—to contain
Sheryl Swoopes.*

Austin, which had a strong women's basketball program. But Swoopes was very close to her family, especially her mother, Louise, and after three days in Austin, she became so homesick, she returned to Brownfield.

Swoopes enrolled at South Plains College, a two-year college in Levelland, Texas. At South Plains, Swoopes immediately made her mark. She led the team to a 27-9 record during her freshman year and was named junior college

All-American. In her sophomore season, the team finished 25-4, and Swoopes was the MVP of the Western Junior College Conference. At South Plains, Swoopes set 28 records, including most points in a game (45), season (894), and career (1,620). She also averaged 25.3 points per game, a career record, and in her sophomore season had a remarkable 139 steals.

But junior college was not the big leagues. Sheryl wanted to play against the best, but she also wanted to be close to home. So she choose Texas Tech in Lubbock, just 32 miles from Brownfield and near enough to get a home-cooked meal now and then. Before Swoopes arrived at Texas Tech, the school's women's basketball program was a solid one but always seemed to be overshadowed by the University of Texas Lady Longhorns. Now, with Swoopes on board, things were about to change.

Almost immediately Texas Tech became a prominent power. In Swoopes's junior year, the team finished 27-5, won the Southwest Conference, and was invited to the NCAA tournament. In the tournament, the Lady Raiders made it to the West Regional semifinals before being eliminated by Stanford, 75-63. Swoopes averaged 21.6 points a game during the season and was named to two All-American teams.

The coach of the Texas Tech Lady Raiders, Marsha Sharp, acknowledged Swoopes' impact on her program. "We can compete on a national scale because of her," Sharp said. "She'll be a legend in women's basketball, but not just because of her play. She has the charisma that the crowd loves."

And when crowds for Lady Raiders' games at Municipal Coliseum in Lubbock got to see their new star in action, her charisma was quickly recognized. Chants of "Swooooopes!" began to echo regularly through the arena during Tech games. But what Lady Raiders fans experienced during Swoopes junior year was just a taste of even better things to come.

In the summer between her junior and senior years, Swoopes made playing on the U.S. women's basketball 1992 Olympic team a goal. But just before the Olympic trials, she hurt her knee and had to undergo arthoscopic surgery, thus ending any chance she had to play in the 1992 Games.

Her knee, however, healed in plenty of time for what was to become a magical season for Swoopes and the Lady Raiders. During the 1992-1993 season, Swoopes averaged over 26 points per game, but, like her idol, Michael Jordan, she saved her best play for crunch time: the post-season. The team record was 31-3, and once again they were Southwest Conference champs. In the SWC tournament championship game in Dallas' Reunion Arena, against the school she had attended for three days, the University of Texas, Swoopes put on an unforgettable show. The Lady Raiders won, 78-71, and Swoopes scored 53 points, the most ever in the Reunion Arena, surpassing the 50-point record set by Larry Bird and Bernard King, and the most points scored by a woman in a Division I game that season.

After the SWC tournament, the Lady Raiders were placed in the NCAA tournament West region. They took the region by beating Washington, Southern California, and Colorado. In their 79-54 win against Colorado, Swoopes scored 36 points, pulled down 10 rebounds, and had 6 steals. Marsha Sharp called her performance "incredible."

Swoopes runs right by Angela Adamoli of Italy in the 1994 Goodwill Games in Moscow. The U.S. won the match, 92-37.

From the West regional, the Lady Raiders headed to Atlanta for the Final Four. Also making the trip to Atlanta was Sheryl's mother. "It's such an honor and a thrill to be here," said Louise Swoopes, who previously had never left the state of Texas. With two of Sheryl's brothers accompanying her, Louise drove 19 hours from Brownfield to Atlanta to be with her daughter during her big weekend.

In the semifinal game, Texas Tech was matched against Vanderbilt, which was ranked number one in the country. But the Lady Raiders' choking defense held Vandy to just 46 points, and Tech won, 60-46. Again, the star of the game was Sheryl Swoopes, who scored 31 points, had 11 rebounds, 3 steals, and 2 blocked shots. "Sheryl pretty much took over the game," said her teammate, center Cynthia Clinger. "But we pretty much expect her to do that."

In the final, the Lady Raiders were pitted against Ohio State, and the Swoopes show was on. In the first half of the game, she scored 23 points, a record for a half in a championship game. The record did not last long, however, because in the second half Swoopes went out and scored 24. Throughout the game, she was virtually unstoppable, hitting 16 of 24 from the field, 4 three-point shots, and a perfect 11 for 11 at the free-throw line. The Lady Raiders won, 84-82, but the game was not as close as the score indicated.

A dejected Nancy Darsch, head coach of Ohio State, explained how she tried to stop Swoopes. "We had made some plans to contain her," Darsch said. "We wanted to rotate people on her, which we did. We wanted her to work hard for her shots and not just get lay-ups. We also tried trapping her when she had the ball. But she answered everything we tried. You don't appreciate Sheryl Swoopes until you have to stop her."

Swoopes admitted that she was in a scoring "zone" during the game. "I just felt I needed to score whenever I got the ball," Swoopes said. "At times, I get in my mind that I just can't miss."

"That was one of the best performances in history," said Nancy Lieberman-Cline, the former women's basketball great who was broadcasting the game for CBS radio. "She's just taken the history of the game to the next level. How do I talk about her without ruining my own legend?"

When it was all over, Swoopes set 10 Final Four records, including the 47 points in the final, the most ever scored in an NCAA basketball championship game, women's or men's. Other impressive NCAA tournament records Swoopes set included the total of 177 points she scored in the five games of the tournament and her scoring average of 35.4 points.

Swoopes recognized that though she was the dominant player, basketball is a team sport and everyone contributed. It was the real reason why the Lady Raiders were champs. "All this Sheryl Swoopes uproar draws attention away from my teammates," Swoopes said. "I'm surrounded by such great players that I just try my best to be better than they are."

After the season, the accolades for Swoopes started to pile up. Some of her awards included tournament MVP, Kodak All-American, Naismith Trophy winner for being women's basketball Player of the Year, Broderick Cup winner as collegiate female Athlete of the Year, and *Sports Illustrated* female Player of the Year.

After all the awards and the thrill of winning a national championship, the inevitable letdown occurred for Swoopes. There was almost nowhere else for her to play. Swoopes did have an option others of earlier generations never had, and that was to play in Europe. She was offered a contract to play for a women's team in Bari, Italy. For a teenager who was homesick going to a school in her own state, traveling and living in another country seemed to be even more traumatic. Yet Swoopes went to play for Bari.

"I didn't even like pasta, really until I got there," Swoopes said at the time. "Now I do because I don't have a choice. It's all they have."

But the Italy experience only lasted three months. Swoopes was averaging 23 points a game when she left the team because she wasn't being paid. Once again, Swoopes, at just 22 years old, was without a league.

In 1996, she was named to the U.S. women's basketball team to compete in the Olympics. The Games took place in Atlanta, the city where Swoopes made history three years earlier.

With a strong, well-balanced team, Coach Tara Van Derveer did not need Swoopes to score 40 or 50 points. She made sure all her players got into the game—and the U.S. team won the gold medal easily.

After the U.S. set a record by beating Zaire, 107-47, Sheryl Swoopes summed up her team's emotions, "Off the court, we may feel pity or sorrow for other coaches because they're not as fortunate as we are," she said. "But this is all about business."

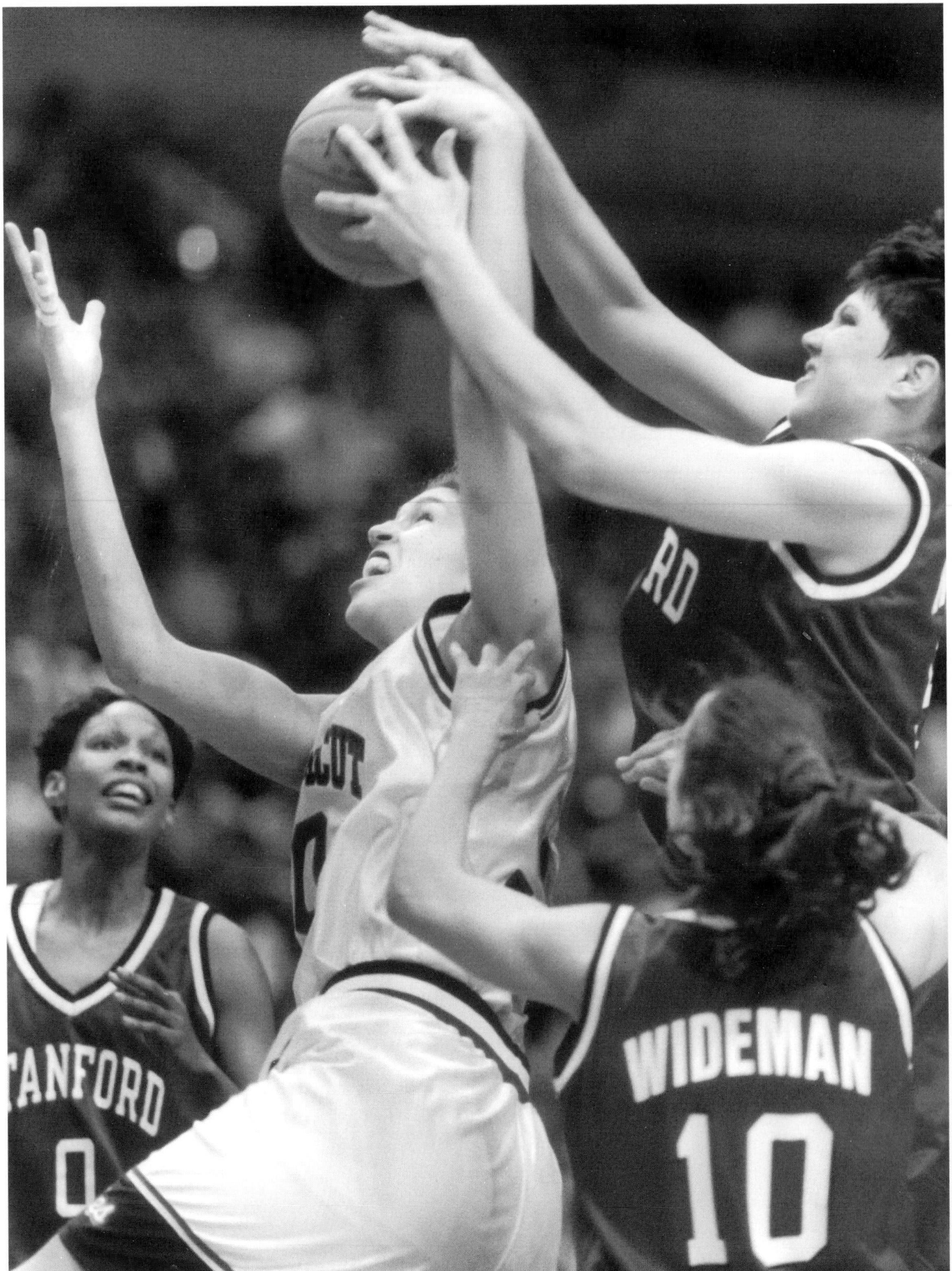
STANFORD
WIDEMAN
10

5

REBECCA LOBO: THE CELEBRITY

In Spanish, *lobo* means *wolf*. But during Rebecca Lobo's sophomore season at the University of Connecticut, head women's basketball coach Geno Auriemma thought the play of his prized recruit from the year before was anything but wolf-like. Lobo had a good freshman year at UConn, being named Big East Rookie of the Year with a scoring average of 14.3 points per game along with 7.9 rebounds. Still, Auriemma wasn't satisfied. Statistics, he felt, can be hollow. "You have to take the last shot. You have to get the big rebound. You have to block the shot," Auriemma preached to Lobo. He wanted her to do more than just put up good numbers. He wanted her to set an example to her teammates. He wanted her to become a leader. To

Rebecca Lobo takes on three players from Stanford University but comes away with the rebound.

get tough. To show more wolf-like ferocity on the court.

Nastiness, however, just wasn't in Rebecca Lobo's nature. Growing up in a household in Southwick, Massachusetts, that her mother, Ruth Ann, claimed was right out of the television show "The Waltons," was not the background for the ferocity Auriemma was seeking. But being the youngest of three children, with her older brother and sister both excellent athletes who involved her in their fun and games, bred inner strength and toughness. And when her older brother, Jason, used to organize boxing matches between Rebecca and her sister, Rachel, that toughness began to take form. "I'd put mittens on them, get on my knees and referee," Jason Lobo said. "If I got them mad enough, they'd box till one of them cried, then I'd spend the next 20 minutes telling them why they couldn't tell Mom."

The children didn't only box, they played all sports together. In the Lobo family, basketball became the sport of choice. Jason, six years older than Rebecca, grew to 6' 11" and went on to play hoops at Dartmouth, while Rachel, two years older, played at Salem State in Massachusetts. It was only natural that Rebecca, at 6' 4", would also drift toward basketball.

At Southwick-Tolland Regional High School, in her first basketball game as a freshman, Lobo scored 32 points. In one high school game, she scored 62 points and was asked how she felt. "Embarrassed," was her answer. "I mean this is a team game."

Her high school coach, Jim Vincent, was impressed with her quiet leadership abilities. "She demonstrates such great sportsmanship on and off the court that members of the other team even look up to her," said Vincent.

As a high school senior in 1991, Lobo was selected as a First Team All-American by *USA Today*, Gatorade, *Street & Smith Magazine*, and Converse. She was also 1991 Massachusetts Player of the Year. Her scoring average was 29.7 points per game, and over her high school career she scored 2,710 points, the most ever scored by a Massachusetts high school player, female or male. With those types of numbers, colleges were clamoring for her services.

Though she visited numerous schools, she made her mind up early that UConn was her choice. "When I took my official visit, I definitely knew I wanted to come to Connecticut," said Lobo. She liked the friendly atmosphere on the campus but was most impressed by UConn women's basketball coach, Geno Auriemma. "He was the key," she said. "I liked his sense of humor."

Coach Auriemma wasn't being funny when he challenged Lobo in the middle of her sophomore season at UConn. "We're at a crossroads," Auriemma told her. "I can't reach you. If you want to leave, fine."

Lobo definitely did not want to leave. Instead, she reexamined her role on the team and decided to take the advice of her coach. "Coach was right in what he said I needed to do," Lobo said. "I picked up the intensity and got a little mean."

Lobo celebrates along with teammates Kara Wolters (number 52) and Pam Weber (number 32) after beating Virginia in the 1995 NCAA tournament.

After their heart-to-heart talk, Lobo did change. She assumed the role of team leader and, according to Auriemma, "learned what it was like to have to carry a team."

That sophomore year, she was named Honorable Mention All-America and First Team All-Big East. Playing forward for the Huskies, Lobo averaged 16.7 points and 11.2 rebounds per game. Her 93 blocked shots were a team record and ranked fifth in the NCAA in that department. For the 1992-93 season, the UConn women finished with a 18-11 record and lost in the first round of the NCAA tournament to Louisville.

Lobo was beginning to establish herself as a dominant player, not only for the Huskies but in the nation. And in her junior year, she began to take control, showing that she was one of the top women players in the country.

Lobo, who became women's basketball's biggest celebrity, signs autographs at Spalding's headquarters. She signed an endorsement deal with the sporting goods company and served on their basketball advisory staff.

In the meantime, Coach Auriemma was putting the pieces of the puzzle together. He was assembling a Husky team that would go on to make history. The team started their rise during the 1993-1994 season, when they won the Big East championship and advanced to the final eight of the NCAA Tournament. Their season record was a very impressive 30-3, and their leader, unquestionably, was Rebecca Lobo.

Finishing the season with a 19.2 per game scoring average, 11.2 rebounds, and a total of 131 blocked shots, Lobo was named First Team All-American in 1993-1994, but the season was not without its bumps. In the Big East Tournament semifinals, Lobo fractured her nose. The setback, however, didn't stop her from playing against Seton Hall in the final. Wearing a protective guard on her nose, Lobo went out and scored 17 points, pulled down 9 rebounds, and blocked 4 shots in the Huskies' 77-51 win.

The broken nose paled next to the trauma Lobo experienced earlier that junior season. Just after a big Husky win against Virginia, Lobo's mother, Ruth Ann, learned that she had breast cancer. She wouldn't let Rebecca get down and told her to keep playing hard. "You do your job and I'll do mine," Ruth Ann said, determined to recover.

And that was just what Rebecca did. Knowing that her mother was fighting a tougher battle than she could ever imagine gave Rebecca even more strength and a positive outlook. "Petty things don't bother me as much as they used to," Rebecca said at the time.

While she was excelling on the basketball court, Lobo was also distinguishing herself in the classroom. It's not easy to juggle the demands of school with the hectic schedule of big-time college basketball, but Lobo found a way. A political science major, Lobo made the Dean's List every semester at UConn, and with her 3.7 grade point average was selected to numerous academic All-American teams.

Lobo's mother credits her daughter's self-discipline for her dual success in basketball and academics. "Rebecca has the best self-discipline of anyone I know," Ruth Ann Lobo said. "Whether it's in athletics or academics, when she makes a commitment, she gives her all."

And where did Lobo get that self-discipline? "It definitely comes from my parents," Rebecca said. "They have always let me know that if you have committed yourself to doing something, that not only are you going to do it, but you are going to do it as well as you can."

For a team to win, however, it takes more than one player to display commitment and self-discipline. On the cover of the team's media guide before the 1994-1995 season was the slogan "One Team. One Goal." It was what Coach Auriemma would constantly preach to his players to keep them focused. But a coach also needs leadership on the court, and for that, Auriemma turned to his senior star, Rebecca Lobo.

As the Huskies ripped through the regular season, outscoring opponents by an average margin of an incredible 33 points, Lobo was once again displaying All-American skills. She averaged 17.3 points a game, 10.3 rebounds, 3.4 blocks, and 3.8 assists. But it was the little things—the things that didn't show up in statistics—that impressed most people. "She makes everybody else on her team better," said one of her opponents, St. John's forward Lynn Lattanzio.

"What is she great at?" asked Coach Auriemma. "I can't say any one thing. But the sum of all the parts is unreal."

In two of UConn's tougher games during the season, playing against 17th-ranked Kansas and number-one-ranked Tennessee, Lobo combined for 38 points, 20 rebounds, 10 assists, and 7 blocks. By the end of the season, Lobo had shattered numerous Connecticut records and had become the school's all-time leading rebounder (1,268) and shot blocker (396).

But individual records were not the point. It was "One Team. One Goal." The Huskies finished the regular season undefeated, only the sixth team in Division I women's hoops to do so. It was a remarkable achievement, but the team's ultimate goal was to win a national

In 1995, President Bill Clinton invited Rebecca Lobo and her brother Jason to go for a jog together in Washington, D.C.

championship, and the Huskies still had work to do to attain that goal.

The road toward the championship started with Connecticut's 85-49 win against Seton Hall in the Big East tournament. After the win, the Huskies were awarded a number one seed in the NCAA Tournament and placed in the East region, with all their games to be played at Gampel Pavilion on the UConn campus in Storrs, where there would be over 8,000 rabid Husky fans in attendance.

The first three games of the tournament were wipeouts; UConn demolished Maine, Virginia Tech, and Alabama. Their next game, a 67-63 squeaker over Virginia, was their closest of the season. With the win, UConn advanced to the Final Four in Minneapolis, Minnesota.

In the semifinals, the Huskies were paired against Stanford, and UConn returned to form by winning easily, 87-60. Lobo scored 17 points and had 9 rebounds in the victory. The winner of the other semifinal was Tennessee. In the final the next day, UConn matched up against a team they had beaten earlier in the season, but one whom many believed was better. Despite their undefeated season, there were skeptics who believed UConn was overrated, that they played a soft schedule. One of those included the coach of the Stanford Cardinal, Tara Vanderveer, whose team UConn had just demolished. "Tennessee is going to win tomorrow," Vanderveer predicted.

"People had a lack of respect for us," said UConn guard Jennifer Rizzotti. So the Huskies had something to prove. They wanted the world to know their record was no fluke. It was what UConn needed; a little more fuel to add to their fire.

In the first half, the Huskies struggled. Tennessee was leading by six, and both Lobo and UConn center Kara Wolters were in foul trouble. But Coach Auriemma wasn't worried and didn't want his team to get down. At halftime, he pumped them up, reminding them how good they were. He also had to whisper a few tough words to his star. "You're player of the year, MVP," he said. "If you play bad, everything you have done for the last six months is down the tubes. No one is going to believe it. They're not going to remember it."

But no one would forget the show Lobo put on in the second half. After the intermission, she began hitting shots from both inside and out, taking over the game. "I just felt really confident," Lobo said. "I felt I could take the game into my own hands."

"We want her to want the ball," said Jennifer Rizzotti. "We want her to win the game for us. That's what she's supposed to do."

And that is exactly what she did. Lobo's resurgence helped spark the Huskies to a comeback 70-64 victory. They were a perfect 35-0 and national champions. Coach Auriemma was beaming after the win and proud of his senior star who scored a team high, 17 points and 8 rebounds, and was named Most Outstanding Player of the Tournament. "In the biggest showcase of her life she rose up and got it done," he said.

"Lobo did what she had to do," conceded losing Tennessee coach, Pat Summit. "She made huge plays."

Lobo's trophy case got very crowded after her senior season. Some of her new hardware included the Naismith Player of the Year, the Honda Cup National Player of the Year, Wade

Trophy recipient, ESPY Award, and Associated Press Player of the Year. She also became a media darling with appearances on "David Letterman," "Regis & Kathie Lee," and "CBS This Morning." But the next biggest thrill for Lobo, after winning the national championship, might have been her personal visit with the President of the United States.

During the season, when the team was playing Georgetown in Washington, D.C., Coach Auriemma took his team to the White House, but found both the front and back doors locked. So after winning the championship, President Clinton invited the Huskies to the White House for a return visit. "Maybe this time we'll come through the front door!" Coach Auriemma joked.

The team met with the President in May, but Lobo couldn't make the trip because of a commitment with the 1995 U.S. Women's National team. To make it up to her, President Clinton invited her to come on her own. And a month after her teammates met the President, Lobo visited the White House. "I was just sitting there waiting in a room with a couple of people and he came down without anyone around him in his jogging clothes and came over yawning," said Lobo of the President. "He seemed like a normal human being that just got out of bed and was about to go for a jog. He made me feel real comfortable. It was almost like I had to hit myself a couple of times and say 'this is the President of the United States.'"

One of Lobo's future goals is to raise awareness of women's basketball throughout the country. Going for a jog alongside the President of the United States was a good start.

AFTERWORD

Before the 1996 Olympics in Atlanta, the U.S. women's basketball team traveled over 100,000 miles, crossing the globe to scrimmage against the best teams. Coming into the Olympic games, they had won over 50 games and lost none.

The U.S. male basketball team, nicknamed the "Dream Team III," was expected to be the favored of the two. But once the women arrived and began playing, the crowds went wild. The women managed to keep up the incredible momentum they had had on the road and, like the men, brought home the gold medal.

Their success sparked something in the public and the dream of a women's professional basketball league was realized. The United States joined the trend in Europe, Asia, and South America in supporting its own professional female leagues—the American Basketball League and the Women's National Basketball Association.

The American Basketball League, or ABL, consists of 99 players, including seven members of the powerful 1996 U.S. Olympic gold medal team, among them, Jennifer Azzi, Dawn Staley, and Teresa Edwards. The nine teams comprising the ABL, tipped off in October 1996. The Columbus Quest defeated the Richmond Rage in three games of a five-game series in early March 1997 to win the first ABL title. Beginning in the fall of 1997, ABL games will be televised on the Fox network and viewership is expected to be in the tens of millions.

Divided into an Eastern and Western Conference, the Women's National Basketball Association (WNBA) includes eight teams. Sheryl Swoopes of the Houston Comets and Rebecca Lobo of the New York Liberty were among the first signed by their respective teams. They were joined by some of the most talented women in the game, including Lisa Leslie, Cynthia Cooper, and Ruthie Bolton-Holifield.

Since June 21, 1997, over a million people have attended a WNBA game and millions more have tuned into the games on television. The WNBA's inaugural season ended with a bang on August 30, 1997, when the Houston Comets defeated the New York Liberty.

The first professional women's basketball players of the ABL and WNBA will long be remembered for their efforts, victories, and determination on the court, and they can be called pioneers in their own right. However, they owe a large part of their professional careers to the women who played basketball at a time when it was only intended for men—women like Ann Meyers and Nancy Lieberman-Cline, whose incredible stories will continue to be told to future generations of eager young women.

STATISTICS

	G	FGM	FGA	PCT	FT%	RBD	AST	ST	BL	PT	AVG
Ann Meyers UCLA, 1975-1978	97	693	1386	500	78.5	819	544	403	na	1685	17.4
Nancy Lieberman Old Dominion, 1976-1980	134	972	2430	472	75.7	1167	961	286	40	2430	18.1
Cheryl Miller USC, 1982-1986	128	1159	2331	497	76.4	1534	615	462	331	3018	23.6
Sheryl Swoopes South Plains, 1990-1991 Texas Tech, 1992-1993	130	1263	2536	498	78.2	1299	805	527	na	3265	25.1
Rebecca Lobo University of Connecticut, 1992-1995	126	837	1680	498	69.5	1268	260	na	396	2133	16.9

G	games
FGM	field goals made
FGA	field goals attempted
PCT	percent
FT%	free-trow percentage
RBD	rebounds
AST	assists
ST	steals
BL	blocks
PT	points
AVG	average
NA	not available

SUGGESTIONS FOR FURTHER READING

Anderson, Kelli. "Rhymes With Hoops," *Sports Illustrated*, April 12, 1992.

Kirkpatrick, Curry. "The Game Is Her Dominion," *Sports Illustrated*, December 3, 1979.

Lieber, Jill. "Stars of State, Screen, and Court", *Sports Illustrated*, April 9, 1984.

Lieberman-Cline, Nancy, and Debbie Jennings. *Lady Magic.* Champaign, Il: Sagamore Publishing. 1993.

Lobo, Ruth Ann and Rebecca Lobo. *The Home Team.* New York; Kodansha Publishers, 1996.

Shea, Jim. *Husky Mania.* New York: Villard Publishers, 1995.

Telander, Rick. "The Post With the Most," *Sports Illustrated*, March 13, 1995.

Steve Wulf. "A Girl Who's Just One of the Guys," *Sports Illustrated*, July 21, 1980

INDEX

ABOUT THE AUTHOR

J. KELLY is a free-lance writer based in New York City who writes frequently about baseball and basketball. He is also the author of *Clyde Drexler* in Chelsea House's "Basketball Legends" series.

PICTURE CREDITS

UPI/Bettmann: pp. 2, 12, 18, 27; AP/Wide World: pp. 6, 9, 15, 21, 24, 28, 31, 34, 37, 40, 43, 50, 53, 54, 57; Archive Photos: p. 46.